SELF-PORTRAIT: MARGOT ZEMACH

SELF-PORTRAIT:

Margot Zemach

written and illustrated by Margot Zemach

▲▼ ADDISON-WESLEY

Text and illustrations Copyright © 1978 by Margot Zemach
All Rights Reserved
Addison-Wesley Publishing Company, Inc.
Reading, Massachusetts 01867
Printed in the United States of America
ABCDEFGHIJK-WZ-798

Book designed by Charles Mikolaycak

Library of Congress Cataloging in Publication Data

Zemach, Margot.
Self portrait.

SUMMARY: A well-known illustrator of children's
books talks about herself, her life, and her work.
1.   Zemach, Margot — Juvenile literature.   2.   Illustra-
tors — United States — Biography — Juvenile literature.
[1.   Zemach, margot.   2.   Illustrators]   I.   Title.
NC975.5.Z45A4   1978   741'.092'4 [B] [92]   78-17140
ISBN 0-201-09096-1

"I love so much seeing, I live with my eyes."
Oskar Kokoschka

I was born in 1931 in Hollywood; it was the time of the great depression and almost everyone was out of work, hungry and on the move. My mother worked as an extra in the movies when she could get a job, while I went traveling back and forth across America with my mother's sister Margie, her husband Tom, their big dog Pam, and a white cat. We sold ink eradicator door to door. I remember the signs and telephone poles marking our way, and the road spilling out in front of the car. I was two when we stopped in Oklahoma City, where my grandparents lived in a serious, stucco house.

After awhile Margie and Tom moved on, but I stayed behind. Both my grandparents were doctors and so was my grandmother's sister Aggie, who lived with them. My uncle Charles, who played the clarinet and was too young to be a doctor, lived there, too. On Sunday my grandfather read me the comics and smoked a big cigar. I thought that Mickey and Minnie Mouse lived in our squeaky radio and that, if only I could get inside, I would see them dancing in a tiny city of tubes and lights.

After Charles, my best friend was Baron the dog. We spent our time in the backyard in the mud and water, digging holes to go to China and burying dead birds. I often dreamt about a wolf who stood outside my window looking at me. His eyes were red and his body was made of raw meat — steaks, ribs and chops. For awhile I went to dancing school with other girls who had hopes of becoming Shirley Temple. But at the school recital my shoulder strap broke, and I forgot the little I knew about dancing and wished myself at home in the mud. It was obvious to me that I would never be Shirley.

When I was five, I went to live in New York City with my mother and stepfather Benjamin.

The lights of the city were the most beautiful thing I had ever seen.

Because both my parents worked in the
theater, Benjamin as a dancer and director
and my mother as an actress, the theater
became a big part of my life. It was a
place of great magic where anything
could happen. How rich to be out late at
night, to explore the cavernous back-
stages with their painted sets of castles or
city streets stacked against the walls, and
the racks of bright costumes — Gypsy
skirts, wedding gowns, silver wings —
and glittering glass jewels. I loved the
laughter best and being where I could
see the dances and plays take shape. The
transformation of my parents onstage was
an endless source of amazement to me.
Was the man sitting at the dinner table
reading the newspaper and eating lettuce
really the same person who last night
onstage had been a leaping demon or a
camel or a soldier?

13 Once backstage I was approached by an ancient, very ragged woman who began poking at me and pinching my arm, all the while cackling horribly. I was getting pretty worried, fearing her to be an escaped witch before I recognized, just slightly, in her cackling the voice of my usually beautiful mother.

I learned to roller-skate, cook on a hot plate and be by myself. I first remember drawing while waiting for something else to happen, but probably by the time I was five or six, I was drawing because I wanted to tell myself stories or jokes.

If there are only cornflakes and mustard in the kitchen, it's a great thing to be able to paint chocolate pudding.

GIRLS

We moved around the city, and I went to many schools, hating every minute, a miserable prisoner from nine to three. When I was fourteen, the girls in my school grew up fast. I was awed by their bosoms and bubblegum. After my sister Amielle was born, we moved to Hollywood where I finished high school and had all sorts of jobs. Once I worked as an usherette at Grauman's Chinese Theater. But I was blind in the dark and couldn't even see where I was going, let alone find seats for hordes of furious, impatient people. I stumbled about getting myself tangled in the heavy curtains and stepping on the customers' feet, but worst of all, I seated a lot of people on top of each other. I left with dignity before I could be fired. After failing as an usherette, a typist, salesperson, messenger and file clerk, I decided to go to art school.

At that time I wanted to become a famous artist whose work would hang in museums, and it worried me that no matter how serious I was trying to be, everything I drew looked funny. After a few years of determined effort, I could draw fairly seriously when I wanted to, and I was granted a Fulbright Scholarship to study drawing in Vienna.

The first night there I met another Fulbright student named Harve Fischtrom. Harve had always gotten A's in school, and he played the violin. He knew about philosophy and history and could put all sorts of ideas together in ways that made exciting good sense. He thought that making pictures was great, and I thought that his way of thinking was marvelous. We had a very idyllic life that year; I didn't go to school, and neither did he. We talked all the time and walked all over the city. We went to coffee-houses, concerts and marketplaces, and I made big serious pictures.

At the end of the year we sailed sadly back to America where I became a receptionist at a clinic in California, and Harve became a graduate student in Massachusetts. We spent so much time writing to each other that we decided to get married. We were jobless, broke and expecting a baby when we sold our first children's book about a boy in Vienna. Harve wrote the story, and I drew the pictures. Though his main interest was teaching, every year after that Harve either wrote or adapted a story for me to illustrate, and because we were best friends, we worked well together. Kaethe was born in 1958.

Three books and two years later, our second daughter, Heidi, was born. Illustrating books turned out to be a good way for me to make a living while rocking a baby bed with one foot. Much more than that, I can create my own theater and be in charge of everything. When there is a story I want to tell in pictures, I find my actors, build the sets, design the costumes and light the stage. I know that when I am done, all I will ever have is black lines on paper, but if I can get it all together and moving, it will come to life. The actors will work with each other, and the dancers will hear the music and dance. When the book closes, the curtain comes down. Rachel was born in 1962.

HEIDI-1960

When Rachel was six years old, we felt 20
that it was time to go out and see the
world again, so we sold everything and
set off with the passports and children to
have some adventures and find a larger
place where we could live more cheaply.
As to school, we thought we would teach
the children ourselves.

We went to England, Denmark, Austria, Italy. We had adventures, but after awhile, we needed a place to sit down. We stayed for a few months in Italy, where the hills were covered with red poppies and bald chickens squawked under the cherry trees. Lizards lived in our house, and the sun shone uproariously, but no lessons were done, and it was time to be serious again.

When Shlemiel Went to Warsaw

AWAKE AND DREAMING

25 For the next year we lived on a chicken farm in Denmark, and the children took the train to a good school near Copenhagen. All winter the sky was low overhead, heavy and gray, but in April the sun began to shine, and our fourth daughter Rebecca was born.

LONDON 1970 - 1975

A PENNY A LOOK

AUNTIE

MR. A.L. LLOYD

DUFFY AND THE DE

REBECCA

Duffy
and The Devil

For the next five years we lived in a narrow, four-story house near Greenwich Park in Southeast London. We made some good friends and sometimes we traveled a bit to Scotland and Wales, but for the most part, we worked on books. The children went to school, and Rebecca learned to walk and talk. We all felt that London was our home and neighborhood.

In November, 1974 Harve died. Goodby to my best friend, the end of talking and being parents together.

London DEC 1974

For three years, the children and I have been living in an old house in Berkeley, California. Besides being a mother every day, I am working on books because it is my job. It not only buys us shoes and toothpaste but is a real privilege and a pleasure.

The pictures in this book incorporate scenes and characters from other books by Margot Zemach. They show what she was creating at her drawing board, books, in the midst of what she was creating away from it, her family. Together, she says, they form a true composite portrait of the artist, up to the present.

The characters and scenes include: The giant from *Salt, An Afanaseu Story*, adapted by Harve Zemach from a translation by Benjamin Zemach. (Page 18)

The grandpa and grandma from *The Speckled Hen*, adapted by Harve Zemach. (Page 19)

Mommy, Buy Me A China Doll, An Ozark Folksong, adapted by Harve Zemach. (Page 21)

The buildings and people from *When Shlemeil Went To Warsaw*, by Isaac Bashevis Singer. (Page 22)

The Judge and The Horrible Thing from *The Judge*, by Harve Zemach. The buildings and people from *Mazel And Shlimazel*, or The Milk Of A Lioness, by Isaac Bashevis Singer. (Page 23)

The lovers, the countryside and the villains from *Awake and Dreaming*, by Harve Zemach. (Page 24)

The Redheaded Rascal and the Lazy Good-for-Nothing brothers from *A Penny A Look*, by Harve Zemach. Duffy and the Devil dancing, from *Duffy And The Devil*, adapted by Harve Zemach. (Page 26)

Squire Lovel out on the moors (of Greenwich Park) with one of his dogs (really the Zemach's Poppa Dog, who appears frequently in Margot Zemach's books) just after the squire's clothes have turned to ashes — from *Duffy And The Devil*. The figure in the background, who is throwing a ball to the dog, is Margot Zemach herself. She had just learned that *Duffy And The Devil* had been awarded the Caldecott Medal. (Page 27)

The statue in Greenwich Park was the model for the king in *The Princess And The Froggie*, by Harve and Kaethe Zemach. (Page 28)

The cow from *It Could Always Be Worse*, adapted by Margot Zemach. Visible behind Kaethe, Heidi and Rachel are their reflections as Gladys, Hilda and Rose in *To Hilda For Helping*, which is a true story, by Margot Zemach. (Page 30–31)

Margot Zemach has illustrated more than 30 books for children and has received every major award conferred in this field, including two Caldecott Honor Awards for *The Judge* and *It Could Always Be Worse*, and the Caldecott Medal for *Duffy And The Devil*.